PRAYER HIKE

Mindful
Encounters
with God
During Life's Adventures

By Karen Sinclair

PRAYER HIKE

Prayer Hike

MINDFUL ENCOUNTERS WITH GOD DURING LIFE'S ADVENTURES

By Karen Sinclair

Published by Karen Sinclair

PRINT EDITION

ISBN: **0981450547**
ISBN-13: **978-0981450544**
CATALOGUING DATA
Sinclair, Karen
Prayer Hike: Mindful Encounters with God during Life's Adventures
Summary: Praying about modern concerns using scripture as the guide
1.   Christian prayer   2. God's will
PERMISSIONS
THE HOLY BIBLE, NEW INTERNATIONAL VERSION ®,
NIV® COPYRIGHT © 1973, 1978, 1984, 2011 BY BIBLICA,
INC. ® USED BY PERMISSION, ALL RIGHTS RESERVED
WORLDWIDE

———————————————————————

Prayer Hike

© Karen Sinclair

P.O. Box 206
South Orange, NJ 07079
UNITED STATES OF AMERICA

WWW.KARENSWALL.COM

DEDICATION

To the poor in spirit and to those who pray
and care about others

THE LORD'S PRAYER

"Our Father in heaven,

hallowed be your name,

Your kingdom come, your will be done on earth as
it is in heaven.

Give us today our daily bread and forgive us our
debts

as we also have forgiven our debtors.

Lead us away from temptation and deliver us
from evil"
Matthew 6:9-13

ACKNOWLEDGMENTS

This prayer book is inspired. Thanks to God for his revelation of the ageless gems in the Bible that help people who are searching today. I am humbled with gratitude to him for my parents who quietly nurtured good soil in me and discreetly planted durable seeds that continue to burst forth with surprises on my adventures even after my parents are gone. I pray that this hike refreshes you in your own adventures and is pleasing to God.

PREFACE

Prayer is one way that we encounter God. Prayers in this book follow James 5:13-16 which urges us to call out to God in faith whether in trouble or happiness.

Prayers need not be long and repetitive. Following the warning against babbling and expecting to be answered because of our many words (Matthew 6:7), each prayer in this book is short. Accompanying scriptures promote mindfulness and understanding consistent with 1 Corinthians 14:15.

Prayer positions such as closing eyes, clasping hands and kneeling in a quiet place, may help us to pray in the spirit by blocking distractions, but are not themselves prayer. God hears our prayers however we pray, in thought or in spoken words in any language, even in the midst of turmoil. He is supreme and his presence and response to prayers are divine mysteries.

HOW TO USE THIS BOOK

These short prayers to God may resonate with contemporary needs but should not be memorized. They are guides to assist prayer in each person's words. Use the table of contents or browse through prayers for topics that mirror your circumstances and read the prayers.

As you read, remember that the Bible serves as the authority about Christian faith and prayer. Selected scriptures provide biblical perspectives of various topics. Read them in any Bible and be fed. Gain even greater understanding from reading beyond the particular scriptures.

You need not feel alone. For further clarification, seek Churches, advisors and help from Christians. Also, feel welcome to use the website listed in this book to connect with the author.

As a tool in one-to-one counseling and in small groups, Prayer Hike may be used in sessions that provide opportunities to come together, read the book and look up any scriptures in the Bible. Anyone may discern the messages in the Bible and grow in understanding. Get ready to say your own prayers. The role of group leader is to listen and provide guidance and support as needed.

Prayer Hike encourages you to keep records of the things you are thankful for and update these prayer lists of thankfulness. Unburden problems at God's feet and leave them there as you continue to pray with joy, thanksgiving and hopefulness in his mercy.

Be sure to encounter God with your prayers from the spirit. Take courage from Hebrews 10:16 that God calls you just as you are and he writes his law on your heart. He is in you and with you, knows your inmost being and knows what you need before you ask.

You may find these prayer stones and lights useful on your hike:

Prayer Stones, reminders to give thanks:

Prayer Lights, scripture quotations:

Give
Thanks

PRAYING WITH THANKSGIVING

1 Thessalonians 5:16-18 urges us to give thanks always and to keep praying throughout all circumstances. Thanksgiving may be added to each prayer.

When times are difficult, it can feel as if you have nothing to be thankful for. You are urged to write down the things you are thankful for now so that when those tough times come, you could more readily recount your blessings, remember God's presence and find hope.

Why not make it a habit to add a prayer of thanks whenever you pray? The symbol above appears on some pages as a reminder to include thanksgiving. Giving thanks is always appropriate, whether times seem joyful or gloomy.

Read: Daniel 6:10 A habit of Thanksgiving
2 Corinthians 9:11-12 Giving thanks is a service to God

Rejoice always,
pray continually,
give thanks in all circumstances;
for this is God's will for you in Christ Jesus.

1 Thessalonians 5:16-18

TABLE OF PRAYERS

1.   A PRAYER OF THANKSGIVING

Father, God, I give you thanks for your gracious blessings to me: Help me to value each precious gift and use them all as you would have me do. In particular, I thank you today for:

Eyes that see   My voice   My neighbor

Family & Friends   My hands   My feet

The person who patiently taught me to read

. . . .

Ears that hear   Ability to think   . . . .

. . . .

. . . .

. . . .

. . . .

. . . .

. . . .

. . . .

19

. . . .

. . . .

. . . .

. . . .

. . . .

. . . .

. . . .

. . . .

. . . .

. . . .

What are you thankful for? Some items above are filled in to help you get started but blessings are personal and different for each of us. Make your personal list. Delete items above, insert your personal blessings and update from time to time. Counting your blessings could boost your spirit and inspire you during life's adventures.

2. FRIENDS ARE DOING WRONG

. God and Father, Master of All Creation, I pray
for my friends with the same love that I
pray for myself. I confess our weaknesses
and ask that you watch over them with
your understanding grace, give them
wisdom and guidance, forgive their
wrongs, cleanse their souls and keep them
safe in your loving care, as you continue to
keep me from stumbling. AMEN.

Read: 1 John 5:16-21 About prayers for friends
Matthew 10:16 Have a shrewd attitude
Proverbs 12:26 Choose your friends wisely
2 Corinthians 9:7-8 Do generous acts as
your heart inspires
Jude 1:17-24 Persevere shrewdly

3. SOMEONE HAS DIED

God Almighty, Protector of your people in life and
in death, thank you for the life of this
person and for all that they have been and
done and given, especially their love and
friendship. With your infinite goodness,
forgive [*name*]'s trespasses and grant his/
her soul rest in your eternal peace. Let
those who mourn feel your comfort and
grant their grieving hearts a time to heal.
AMEN

Read: Romans 14:8 About God's care for his
people in life and death
Ecclesiastes 3:1-22 Everything has its time
in our lives
Psalm 23:4 About God's presence in the
darkest times
Romans 8:9-11 The spirit gives life
Psalm 147:3 Be comforted

4. SOMETHING GOOD HAS HAPPENED

Munificent God, I thank you for your glorious blessings, goodness and kindness that add beauty and joy to this life. I glorify your name as I express my joy and gratitude for your inestimable love and care. I ask your continued guidance and understanding so that I may use your gifts wisely as you would have me do. Amen

Read: Psalm 30:11-12 Praises for being rescued by God
James 1:17 Everything good is from God
Luke 12:48 About what is required of gifts received
Philippians 4:6 About thanksgiving for peace
1 Thessalonians 5:16-18 Thanksgiving and God's will for you

5. MY PET IS HURT

Mighty God, Creator of Life great and small, I
thank you for the wonder of all your
creation. Help my pet with your mighty
healing power, guide me as I care for my
pet and let us feel the touch of your
supreme mercy on our lowly lives. Amen

Read: Matthew 5:7 Those who care are blessed
Genesis 1:26 Understanding your role and
duty to animals

Give
Thanks

6. I NEED SOMETHING

Loving Benefactor, Divine God, thank you for
those blessings you have already given me.
I recognize that I have not been deserving
and ask your gracious forgiveness for my
failures as your child. You know and
provide my needs before I ask and today,
with gratitude and faith in your surpassing
grace, I humbly ask for

_____

Read: Matthew 6:8 God knows what you need
before you ask
Mark 11:22-25 Placing faith in God as you
pray
Luke 11:9-13 A Fatherly perspective of
responses to prayer
Matthew 24:4 Don't let others mislead you
2 Peter 2:3 Don't be exploited
James 4:3 About your motive
Luke 18:1-8 God's response is just

Give

Thanks

7. I FEEL ANXIOUS AND WORRIED

God of Peace, please hear my call. Through your
merciful compassion, forgive my weakness,
help me to grow and show me how to walk
in your peace. Take away my anxiety, God
of comfort, and fill me with the calm of
your Holy Spirit and with trust in your
provision and your care for my needs.
Amen

Read: Psalm 91 A comforting song
Jeremiah 29:11 God's plans for your
prosperity
Matthew 6:25-29 Worry is futile
Matthew 6:30-34How it helps to make
righteousness a priority
Philippians 4:12Thankfulness in time of
plenty and in want
Matthew 11:28-30 Invitation for those who
are burdened

Give
Thanks

8.   I DON'T KNOW WHAT TO DO

All-Knowing God, inspire my spirit by your
        awesome power, clarify my vision and
        make me ready to follow your light. Guide
        me out of this uncertainty with your perfect
        counsel, to serve your purpose always as I
        purposefully exercise my free will and
        follow the teachings of my Lord and savior,
        Jesus Christ.
        [Wait]
        Amen

Read: John 14:12 Get inspiration from Jesus' work
        1 Corinthians 12:4-5 All kinds of work can
        be in God's service
        1 Corinthians 10:23-24 Appropriate goals
        for your actions
        Matthew 6:1-3 Ambitions to avoid
        Deuteronomy 5:6-22 Activities to avoid
        2 Corinthians 9:6-12 Do generously as your
        heart inspires
        Isaiah 40:28-31 Wait
        1 Corinthians 12:7-12 Use your gifts for the
        common good

"Is not life more than food, and the body
more than clothes?
Look at the birds of the air;
they do not sow or reap
or store away in barns,
and yet your heavenly Father feeds them.
Are you not much more valuable
than they?
Can any one of you by worrying add a
single hour to your life?"

Matthew 6:25-27

Give
Thanks

9. IT SEEMS THAT MY FAMILY DOESN'T CARE

God of Love, thank you for blessing my life with
enduring care. I yearn to forgive my family
and I ask your saving mercy for clear vision
and for a generous, giving spirit, peace and
love as I forgive my family and receive
your forgiveness and care. Help me to love
others as I love myself and inspire me to
recognize people in this world, whoever
they are, who can walk with me this day in
Jesus' name.   Amen

Read: 2 Corinthians 1:3-10 About comfort from
God
Luke 12:52-53 About division among family
members
1 Corinthians 12:21-28 Christians form a
body of members who care
Matthew 12:48-50 Knowing your Christian
family
Matthew 5:43-47 Care beyond family
Matthew 7:12 How to treat others
Matthew 6:9-13 The Lord's Prayer

10. I DON'T UNDERSTAND

Father God, Master and Creator of All Knowledge,
I bow to you and give you thanks for your
perfect love and full understanding. I don't
understand and I am perturbed and
baffled. Lead me, your child, safely, by
your fatherly grace, through this time of
mystery. In your perfect judgment, grant
me those gifts I need to thrive and persist,
fearing no evil in the presence of your most
brilliant light, wisdom and comfort. Amen

Read: James 3:13-17 Different kinds of
understanding
1 Corinthians 13:9-12 Knowledge, without
God, is immature
1 Corinthians 13:2 Without love, even
understanding adds no value
Ephesians 3:14-19 Understanding, the
fullness of God, through faith
James 1:5-6 Ask for understanding
Psalm 23 Goodness and mercy by God's
grace

Give
Thanks

11. I FEEL AFRAID

Omnipotent God, who helped little David to
overcome gigantic Goliath, have mercy and
rescue me from these frightening
circumstances with your matchless, Holy
power. Wipe my fear away and grant me
courage through your divine grace and
majesty in the name of the Father, Son and
Holy Spirit. Amen

Read: 1 Samuel 17:47-50 Facing adversity in
God's name
Psalm 27 A song of strength in God's
salvation
Psalm 23:4 God is a refuge from fear
1 Corinthians 12:4-7 Help for the common
good is available among God's people
through his gifts
Matthew 10:16 About having a shrewd
attitude in the world

Give
Thanks

12. I FEEL SAD

Dear God, I feel sad. Please look down on me
with your majestic patience and
understanding and fill my heart with your
serene peace. Forgive my sadness in this
valley of gloom and lift me up in your
loving, tender care, Almighty God, Lord,
Most High. Amen

Read: Psalm 51:10-12 For renewal of heart and
spirit
Psalm 91 A comforting song
Psalm 34:17-20 The Lord heals the
brokenhearted
1 Corinthians 12:4-5 People are available to
provide various kinds of help through God's
different gifts to them

Give
Thanks

13. NO-ONE SEEMS TO CARE

Mighty, Loving God who gave your son's life that people like me may have hope, I turn to you acknowledging your generous blessings to me and to all mankind. At this moment when I feel as if no-one cares, I ask that you comfort me and help me to feel your divine, caring presence and find solace in your unspeakable love, in Jesus' name. Amen

Read: John 3:16 God loves you
1 Corinthians 12:21-27 & 12 Christians care for each other as one body
1 Corinthians 12:4-7 Support is also available from people through God's various gifts to them
John 15:9-12 Finding joy in loving others
Psalm 23 God's care for you never falters

Give

Thanks

14. I FEEL HURT OR OFFENDED

Forgiving God, I confess that I feel offended and I
ask your gracious help to move beyond
hurt and look kindly on those who hurt me.
I give you thanks for the armor and
protection you provide through your grace
and seek refuge in your unfailing care.
Sooth my hurt and comfort me, in the
name of our loving Savior, Jesus Christ.
Amen

Read: Romans 12:14-21 Respond to offenders
with goodness
Luke 10:30-37 About mercy
Psalm 121 Looking to God for help
John 3:16 Reassurance of safety in God
1 John 4:7 Love comes from God

Give
Thanks

15. I FEEL ALONE

Dear God who designed beauty and created life in
this world, I feel alone. Help me to
recognize your presence, feel your
incomparable touch and know your power
and glory in this world and in my life. Take
away my feelings of loneliness, show me
your people in this world and help me
always to remember that I am part of a
splendor that is bigger than myself,
through the life, death, resurrection and
salvation of Jesus Christ. AMEN

Read: Psalm 23 God is a refuge
Psalm 27:7-14 A call to God
1 Corinthians 12:4-7 Helpful people are
available through God's gifts
1 John 4:4 God's spirit in you
Ephesians 1:11-14 Inheritance of salvation

Give

Thanks

16. MY FRIENDS ABANDON ME

God of Grace and God of Love, bless my friends
and bless me and help me to feel your
comfort and love, knowing that my friends
and I are weak where you are steadfast.
Help me to embrace your diverse blessings
and the full richness of the life you have
laid for me. Amen

Read: Psalm 121 Lift your eyes to God
Hebrews 13:8 God never changes
1 Peter 1:22-25 People change
Jeremiah 29:11-13 God has plans for you
Psalm 27:1-4 Comfort

Also see: I Need a Friend, p. 37

17. I NEED A FRIEND

Miracle-Working God, I humbly seek your
forgiveness for my many missteps and ask
that you bless me with a friend to walk this
valley with me. Amen
[Wait]

Read: Luke 6:32-42 Expect nothing in return for
love
Matthew 7:12 Treat others as you would
like them to treat you
1 Corinthians 12:12-14 You are not alone
Philippians 2:3-7 Be obliging
Luke 18:9-14 Be humble
Proverbs 12:26 Choose friends wisely
Psalm 23 God walks you through dark
days

There are different gifts, but the same Spirit
distributes them. There are different kinds
of service, but the same Lord. There are
different kinds of working, but in all of
them and in everyone it is the same God at
work. Now, to each one the manifestation
of the Spirit is given for the common good.

To one is given through the Spirit a message of
wisdom, to another a message of
knowledge by means of the same Spirit, to
another faith by the same Spirit, to another
gifts of healing by that one Spirit, and to
others miraculous powers, prophecy,
distinguishing between spirits, speaking in
different tongues, and to still others, the
interpretation of tongues. All these are the
work of one and the same Spirit, and he
distributes them to each one, just as he
determines. Just as a body has many parts,
but all its many parts form one body, so it
is with Christ. For we were all baptized by
one Spirit so as to form one body—
whether Jews or others, slave or free—and
we were all given the one Spirit to drink.
So, the body is not made up of one but of
many.

1 Corinthians 12: 4-14

Give

Thanks

18. I FEEL SICK

Omnipotent God who designed our bodies with
healing systems, infused trees and waters
with healing for us; who touched and
healed the sick and who gives knowledge
and skill to your people so that we are
armed to be well; touch me, heal me and
make me well, I ask, in Jesus name,
trusting that my life is yours now, always
and through eternity and your will be done
on earth as it is in heaven. AMEN.

Read: 1 Corinthians 12:7-9 God's various
provisions through people
Mark 2:4-12 Faith and healing
Ezekiel 47:8-9 & 12 Medicines are part of
God's provision
Matthew 26:39 Seek God's will
Acts 4:10 The source of healing power
Matthew 8 Accounts of Christ's healing
Psalm 147:3 Be comforted

19. SOMEONE I KNOW IS SICK

Merciful God, I bow before you with thanks for
your unsurpassed grace and ask that you
ease the suffering of my friend. Forgive
our failures, infuse my friend with your
healing power and make them fully well, I
ask with faith in the name of the Father,
Son and Holy Spirit, believing that our lives
are yours through eternity and your will be
done on earth and in heaven. AMEN.

Read: James 5:14-16 Asking God for healing
Matthew 6:9-13 The prayer Jesus taught
Psalm 121:1-6 Help comes from God
1 Corinthians 12:1-9 About God's gifts for
the common good
Matthew 26:39 God's will is done
Romans 8:28 God's will for the good of
those who love him
Matthew 9 About healing, mercy and
sacrifice
Psalm 147:3 Comfort

20.1 DISLIKE SOMEONE

God of Mercy and Forgiveness, I confess that I
dislike my fellowman. Forgive me through
your infinite mercy. Strengthen me and
refresh my spirit so that I am not puffed up
and I am able to love my neighbor as I
love myself, as I follow the teachings of the
Christ who gave his life for our sins. Amen

Read: Romans 12:3-5Think soberly about yourself
Galatians 5:14Loving others is paramount
1 Peter 2:11-17Doing good is more than
for serving people
1 Corinthians 13 All about love
Galatians 3:26-28 You are equal with
everyone else

21. I'M TEMPTED TO DO WRONG

Merciful God, thank you for the wisdom to know right from wrong. I confess that I feel tempted and need your help to resist. Please give me the strength to turn away from wrong as I know I should. Amen

Read: 1 Corinthians 10:13 God knows your limits
1 Peter 2:9-10 Those chosen to receive God's mercy must proclaim good
James 4:7-10 Submit to God and he will rescue you
Ephesians 6:10-18 God's power is full protection
Matthew 26:41 Be alert to bodily weakness
1 Peter 2:11-17 Doing good serves higher purposes
Matthew 10:16 Be shrewd
1 Corinthians 15:33-34 About bad company

Give
Thanks

22. I NEED HELP

Divine God, Giver of immeasurably more than
what we ask or imagine, I thank you for
the goodness in my life. Please help me
through this challenge, comfort me in the
midst of calamity, protect me and show me
your way, in Jesus' name. Amen
[Be silent]

Read: Isaiah 40:29-31 God increases the power of
those who have hope in him
Psalm 27:1-7 Safety in God
1 John 5:14-15 Help from God
Ecclesiastes 3 Everything has its time in our
lives
Psalm 23 God's goodness in all situations
1 Corinthians 12:27-28 & 7-11 People are
available to Help

The Spirit helps us in our weakness.
We do not know
what we ought to pray for,
but the Spirit himself wordlessly intercedes
for us.
And he who searches our hearts
knows the mind of the Spirit,
because the Spirit intercedes
for God's people
in accordance with the will of God.

Romans 8:26-27

23. I NEED TO MAKE AN APOLOGY

Forgiving God, I am sorry for my mistakes.
Please forgive me, cleanse my heart and
purify my thoughts. I ask your grace and
mercy to mend my relationships. Give me
the courage to take the right actions,
inspire me with the right words to say and
heal those I have hurt as I follow the Holy
Teacher who taught this path to complete
joy. Amen

Read: 1 Corinthians 13:1 Even the most eloquent
speech gains its value from love
John 15:9-13 Why apologize
Matthew 6: 12-15 The Lord's prayer about
forgiveness and deliverance
Mark 12:30-31 What is most important in
life
James 3:1-6 What you say sets the whole
course of your life

24. I HAVE A SECRET

All-Knowing God, help me to live in your light and
do right with the strength of your teachings
and guidance. Forgive my wrongs, cleanse
my thoughts and lead me out of darkness,
fear and shame, I beseech you Lord Judge
of my secrets and my life. Amen

Read: Psalm 139:7-16 No hiding from God
Mark 12:15-17 Responsibilities to God and
to the world
Romans 2:11-16 Equal responsibility for
secrets
Romans 12:17-21 Overcome wrong with
good
1 Peter 2:13-17 Obeying the law also
serves God's purposes

Give
Thanks

25. I AM IN LOVE

God of Unspeakable Glory, your splendid gift of
love makes me utterly joyful and fully
satisfied. I thank you for my life, for hope
and for blessing me so magnificently with
your greatest treasure. Protect this most
prized gift of love and help us in all we do
to serve your highest duty always and
everywhere in your most wonderful name.
AMEN

Read 1 Corinthians 13:1-8 Identifying love
1 Corinthians 13:13 Love is your greatest
attribute
Mark 12:30-31 Loving is your highest duty
Romans 12:9-12 Loving actions
1 John 4:7 All love comes from God

Give

Thanks

26. I DON'T LIKE HOW I LOOK

Dear God, forgive my dissatisfaction and distress.
I thank you for eyes that see and ask for
vision to know and understand the
rightness of your blessings and care them
to bloom into health with the splendor of
your unique design. Give me courage and
wisdom to use my special gifts and share
what I do have for the glory of your
majestic reign as Father, Son and Holy
Spirit forever and ever, Amen.

Read: 1 Corinthians 12:23-25 About different
parts of the body
Matthew 6:25-31 Unmatchable Glory of
God's provision
Matthew 19:21 About perfection
Galatians 3:26-28 No one is better than
you
Romans 12:2 Determine God's will

Give

Thanks

27. I HATE MYSELF

Lord Almighty, King of Glory, I come to you
bowed low with the weight of hate for
myself. Forgive me and help me not feel
this way. Teach me to commit my spirit
into your hands and receive the power of
your goodness and love and whatever it is
that I need to make this loathsome feeling
go away, Amen.
[Wait]

Read: Psalm 24:7-10 Let God in
Psalm 25:1-7 Trust God's guidance
Hebrews 4:13 God knows exactly what you
are thinking
Psalm 51:1-12 Call for God's help
1 John 3:19-20 God is more powerful than
what is in your heart
1 Corinthians 12:27 & 12 You are a vital
part of a bigger body
Psalm 147:3 Take comfort

Also see: I Need Help, p.43

Give
Thanks

28. I AM EMBARRASSED

God of Matchless Grace and Mercy, I feel
embarrassed. I come to you as I am and
ask your gentle leniency that I may go
forward in witness to your love and care.
Take away my burden, lift up my soul,
shield me and give me confidence and
renewed hope. Amen

Read: Psalm 25:1-5 Plea for protection from
shame
1 Peter 2:4-5 God rebuilds flawed lives into
precious treasure
1 Peter 3:13-17 Face critics with goodness
Romans 12:19-21 Overwhelm mockery
with heaps of good
1 Corinthians 13:8 Love defeats all
disapprovals

29. I DON'T LIKE MY SEXUALITY

Magnificent Designer, Creator of all life and
      Master of all mysteries and all knowledge,
      I, your humble creation, bow to confess
      dislike of my sexuality. Forgive my
      simplicity, fill me with understanding and
      help me to thrive and flourish in your care
      with assurance that I have a right to be.
      Father who divinely created complexity
      beyond human comprehension, show your
      willing servant mindful life with peace, love
      and happiness in your will for me. Amen

Read: Psalm 139:13-16 God knows your inmost
      depths
      Proverbs 14:30 Peace and life
      1 John 4:10-12 This is love
      Romans 12:2 Discern God's will for you
      Philippians 4:8-9 Peace follows good
      1 Corinthians 12:4-7 God made all kinds of
      people for collective benefit

30. I HAVEN'T DONE WHAT I SHOULD HAVE

Merciful God, I confess that I have failed to do
what I should and I ask your forgiveness
and your guidance. Direct the resources
that will help me to fulfil your purpose for
my life and grant me courage, strength and
the will to act for the glory of your reign in
goodness and mercy forever and ever.
Amen

Read: Isaiah 40:29-31 God renews those who
stumble and have hope in him
James 5:16 About confession and prayer
Matthew 6:12-15 The Lord's prayer and
forgiveness:
Ecclesiastes 3:9-14 Complete satisfaction is
God's
Ecclesiastes 3:1-8 Ups and downs are
normal seasons of life

If you see any brother or sister
commit a sin that does not lead to death,
you should pray
and God will give them life.
I refer to those whose sin
does not lead to death.
There is a sin that leads to death.
I am not saying
that you should pray about that.
All wrongdoing is sin, and there is sin that
does not lead to death.

1 John 5:16-17

Give

Thanks

31. I HATE MY LIFE

Dear God, I know that the way I am feeling is not
good and I am turning to you for help. I
hate my life and I just don't know what to
do. I thank you for the big, wide world
and the promise of new life and ask that
you hear my suffering. Save me Almighty
God who showed love for the wretched
weak and broken who were still sinners.
Amen.

Read: Romans 5:5-8 There is hope for you in God
Ephesians 2: 11-16 God welcomes you into
a new life with him

Also see: I Want to Change My Life, p. 94
And: I Need Help, p. 43
And: A Prayer of Thanksgiving, p.19

Give
Thanks

32. I DON'T KNOW WHAT TO SAY

Omnipotent God and Savior, forgive my anxiety
and let your spirit speak through me.
Amen
[Wait]

Read: Matthew 10:16-20 About what to expect as
a servant of God
James 3:1-6 Words set the whole course of
life
Romans 8:26 Your Spirit communicates
wordlessly with God
James 5:16 About confession and prayer
Matthew 11:28-30 God's call to you

Give
Thanks

33. I FEEL DISCOURAGED

God of All Hope and All Grace, I bow before you
needing a miracle. Give me courage and
faith to take one more breath, one more
step, moment by moment, day by day,
knowing that this circumstance will give
way to a stronger life. Amen

Read: Psalm 23 God's fruitful guidance through all
situations:
Ecclesiastes 3 Viewing this circumstance in
its time in our lives
Job 33:8-26 Complaining about God's
provisions in your life
Isaiah 40:29-31 God renews strength of
those who put their hope in him
Jeremiah 29:11-13 God's plans for your
prosperity

Give
Thanks

34. I FEEL LOST

Mighty Shepherd, I confess that I feel lost. Have
compassion on me, lead me out of this
darkness and light my path with vision so
that I can find peace and love as I place
my hope in the care of the good shepherd
who rejoices when the lost are found.
Amen

Read: Luke 15:4-7 God will welcome you with joy
John 8:12 Follow God's light
Philippians 4:8 Reflect on wholesome
things
1 Corinthians 12:5-7 Getting Help
1 Peter 2:11-17 Finding your way

Give

Thanks

35. I AM BEING ABUSED

Oh God, whose oaks of righteousness rise from
ashes of grief and despair, lift this abuse
from me, shield me with your loving care
and make me flourish strong and whole.
Wash my stain with your heavenly beauty
and transform this spirit of despair into a
display of your Holy splendor, in the name
of our sovereign, triumphant Lord. Amen

Read: Psalm 121 Help from God
1 Corinthians 12:5-7 Help from people
Matthew 10:16 Adopting a shrewd attitude
Matthew 10:28 Concern for the
destruction of your soul
Psalm 116 1-13 Calling on God in anguish
Romans 12:17-21 About revenge
Isaiah 61:1-3 God transforms pain in his
name
Psalm 147:3 Be comforted

Give
Thanks

36. I'VE LOST MY JOB

Wonderful, Counselor, Mighty God, save me and
help me to move forward from this job loss
with your guidance. Show me a new path
and green pastures, as I place my trust in
your promise of a table of abundance,
goodness and mercy forever and ever.
Amen

Read: Psalm 23 God is the source of fruitfulness
in all situations
Proverbs 4:5-9 & 13 Wisdom and
understanding are crowns of life
Proverbs 4:23-27 Keep heart, speech,
actions and gaze clean
Luke 12:22-26 Value life
2 Thessalonians 3:10-15 Pursue work
diligently
Jeremiah 29:11 God's plans for you
Luke 22:42 Pursue God's will

37. SOMEONE ELSE LOST THEIR JOB

God of All Life, I lift my friend up to you to be blessed by your divine power that provides everything we need. Guide them to walk this new path as a believer in your direction and eternal sovereignty. Amen

Read: 2 Peter 1:3-8 God provides powerful assets for success
Matthew 7:12 Provide the help you would want to receive
Proverbs 14:23 Diligence has more value than talk
Matthew 6:26-39 God provides abundantly
James 2:16-17 What good does your care do?

38. SOMEONE GETS A NEW JOB

Gracious God, we are overjoyed by your goodness
to us. Thank you for this job. Help us to
work with honor, perform superbly and use
the fruit of our labor with wisdom for good.
Most of all, help us to please you, in the
name of the carpenter who saved the
world, Amen.

Read: Colossians 3:23. Work diligently as a
servant of God
Ecclesiastes 9:10 Work while you can
Deuteronomy 6:10-12 Do not forget God
Psalm 127:1-2 Work is futile without God
Galatians 6:8-10 Keep doing what is right
Mark 6:3-4 and Ephesians 2:19-22 A
carpenter does God's work

Give
Thanks

39. IN A NEW HOME

Almighty God, Father of all Mercies, thank you for
this new home. Enter each room, cleanse
and strengthen every atom and every
space. Shield each occupant, dwell with
us, guide us and crown everyone who
enters with your goodness and happiness
all the days of our lives. Amen

Read: Psalm 127:1 God is the foundation of home
Isaiah 32:17-20 God's promise for the
righteous home
Matthew 7:24-25 Establishing your home
on solid ground
Proverbs 24:3-4 Wisdom, understanding,
knowledge and home
Psalm 91 Protection

Give
Thanks

40. SOMEONE IS TRAVELLING

Lord Of All The Earth, give us the confidence to travel this world knowing that our fate is sealed by our faith in you. Continue to protect those at home and those abroad with your power and glory and deliver us safely from evil forever, world without end. Amen

Read: Luke 10:30-37 Compassion is more important than nationality
Proverbs 15:3 God is everywhere
Psalm 139:7-12 God sees everything
John 10:3-5 God cares his people and they do his will everywhere
Proverbs 16:1-9 Our plans and God's steps

When you pray,
do not keep on babbling like pagans,
for they think they will be heard because of
their many words.
Do not be like them,
for your Father knows what you need
before you ask him.

Matthew 6:7-8

41. SOMEONE LOSES HOME OR BELONGINGS

Mighty God who never sleeps, help and protect my friend who is facing this loss. Light the shadows in our paths and, as we strive together, help us to actively honor your many gifts that support a new home and new life for those who place their trust in you. Amen

Read: Psalm 121 Help from God
Ecclesiastes 3 Life has ups and downs
Galatians 6:2 Assist others with their burdens
Proverbs 6:10-11 Inaction leads to losses
Matthew 6:10 Discern God's will
Matthew 22:36-40 Help others as you would yourself
Psalm 27:1-4 Comfort
Psalm 91:1-4 Shelter

Give
Thanks

42. SOMEONE IS FACING FORECLOSURE

Lord of All the Earth, thanks for your innumerable
    miracles. I ask that you comfort and
    reassure my friend at this frightening time
    and fortify our will with understanding,
    direction and resources to thrive as we lean
    on your awesome power to survive this
    calamity. Help us to trust you and embrace
    your will, maker of heaven and earth and
    everything therein. Amen

Read: Daniel 6:10 & 22-23 Pray constantly and
    believe in God's miraculous deeds
    Proverbs 6:10-11 Inaction leads to losses
    1 Corinthians 12:5-7 People are there to
    help as a gift from God
    Matthew 6:8 God knows what you need
    before you ask
    Matthew 10:16 Be shrewd
    Genesis 37:23-24 & Genesis 50:19-20 Trust
    God through adversity
    Jeremiah 29:11 God's plans for your
    prosperity

43. SOMEONE IS FACING ADDICTION

Forgiving God, help your servant to shed this
addiction and find knowledge and
understanding from you. Forgive and heal
him, save him from evil and direct his path
so that he would take each step forward
free from burden, I ask in the name of the
Savior who gives strength to the weary and
power to the weak, Amen.

Read: 1 Corinthians 12:5-7 People are there to
help as a gift from God
Matthew 7:12   Show empathy
1 John 5:16-20 About prayers for others
Matthew 7:1-6 Assess your own challenges
Galatians 6:1 Protect yourself
Isaiah 40:29-31 God strengthens those
who put their hope in him
John 4:14 & 34 Quenching your thirsts
Matthew 22:36-40 The most important
factor

Give
Thanks

44. SOMEONE I LOVE DISAPPOINTS ME

Ever Faithful, Loving God. I thank you for the gift
of love and for my capacity to love
someone who is imperfect. Comfort and
heal me in this time of disappointment and
save my soul from darkness. Shield me and
show me the way to overcome this
disappointment, in the name of the Father,
Son and Holy Spirit, Amen.

Read: Matthew 22:36-40 The most important
considerations
1 Corinthians 13:4-7 Love perseveres
Matthew 10:16 About a shrewd attitude
toward others
1 John 5:16-17 About praying for others
Luke 6:32-38 Showing love to the
disappointing person
Psalm 121:1-2 Look up

Give

Thanks

45. I'VE BEEN BETRAYED

Almighty God in whom I put my trust, lift my pain
and make me whole. Give me wisdom and
understanding to move forward in your
light with goodness, on a path of
forgiveness for those who betray me, I ask
in the name of the Son who was betrayed.
Amen

Read: Matthew 10:16 About a shrewd attitude in
the wider world
Romans 12:19-21 Respond to wrongs with
good instead of taking revenge
Psalm 23 About God's dependability,
safety, comfort for you
Matthew 5:43-47 About loving the enemy
Proverbs 3:21-26 Wisdom keeps you safe

Give
Thanks

46. I'VE FAILED OR LOST

Wonderful Counselor, Father God, forgive me,
help me to learn from my mistakes and
give me the guidance and wisdom I need
to face this situation with trust in your full
Godly armor now and forever. Amen

Read: Genesis 50:20-22 God's infinite
benevolence
Matthew 6:8 God knows what you need
before you ask
Ephesians 6:10-18 Stand strong in peace
2 Timothy 1:7 Fear is not of God
Romans 12:19-21 Greet opposition with
heaps of good
Matthew 10:28 Concern about losing your
soul

47. I'VE BITTEN OFF MORE THAN I COULD CHEW

Merciful Teacher, I confess that I feel overwhelmed. Please rescue me from the burden of my situation and grant my spirit peace. I humbly ask that you forgive my excesses and give me the wisdom to work soberly so that my efforts are not futile and your precious gifts flourish according to your will, in Jesus' name, Amen
[be still]

Read: Psalm 127:1-2 It is folly to work without God
Isaiah 40:29-31 God strengthens those who put their hope in him
Philippians 1:3-11 God ensures that his work gets completed
Romans 12:3 Assess your capabilities soberly
Matthew 11:28-30 Invitation for those who are burdened

Give
Thanks

48. BEFORE AN EXAM

God of All Understanding, Source of All
Knowledge, guide me and direct my
preparation. Be with me during my exam,
help me to perform as a child who knows
Jesus and grant me success, I ask in the
name of the Highest Source of all wisdom,
knowledge and understanding, Amen.

Read: Proverbs 4:5-9 Wisdom and understanding
are crowns of life
2 Peter 1:5-8 Qualities for effective
success
1 Corinthians 13:2 Value love
Proverbs 2:6-8 Source of knowledge and
success

MINDFUL ENCOUNTERS WITH GOD DURING LIFE'S ADVENTURES

Give
Thanks

49. GRADUATION AND OTHER SUCCESS

Benevolent God, Master of the Harvest, I come to you with gratitude at this moment of success. Thanks for your comfort and guidance through the time of preparation and for your walk with me every step of the journey. Continue to be with me and open my eyes so that my service can be fruitful and your will be done now and forever. Amen

Read: Matthew 13:3-9 Levels of understanding affect quality of outcomes
Matthew 13:23 Understanding multiplies success
James 3:13-18 About wisdom and good life
1 Corinthians 1:4-9 Enrichment from God
Proverbs 3:13-18 Precious effects of wisdom

Give

Thanks

50. AWAITING EXAM RESULTS

Lord of All Hopefulness, thank you for persistence through the shadows and uncertainties of this life. I ask your favor to shine on me, comfort me and give me patience as I wait for these results. Stay close to those who examine my work and help me to face your will with the confidence of a child of your love. Amen

Read: Psalm 23 About God's comfort through anxious times
Psalm 27:13-14 Wait to see God's goodness
Isaiah 45:7 God's omnipotent power
1 Corinthians 13:2 Love matters more than an exam result
Psalm 1:1-3 Success comes in its season

God has put the body together,
giving greater honor to the parts
that lacked it,
so that there should be no division
in the body,
but that its parts should have
equal concern for each other.
If one part suffers,
every part suffers with it;
if one part is honored,
every part rejoices with it.

1 Corinthians 12:24-26

Give
Thanks

51. ON RECOVERY FROM ILLNESS

Masterful Healer, Creator and Giver of Life, I give
you thanks for your healing; for the gift of
help I received from your servants; the
science uncovered for healthy living; the
diligence of those who pursued cures,
performed healing acts, shared caring
words and gave of their hearts' bounty,
resources, and God-given talents. To you,
God, giver of all gifts, I lift my heart filled
with gratitude. Amen

Read: Psalm 121 About God as the source of help
1 Corinthians 12:28 About gifts of healing
among God's people
Proverbs 3:7-8 Your actions in your body's
health
Proverbs 12:18 The role of words in
healing
Isaiah 38:14-17 From anguish to health

52. FOR CAREGIVERS

Benevolent King and Protector on High, watch
over those who serve you with hands and
hearts and heads, bringing hope and
healing to those in need on this earth. We
offer our thanks to them and our hearts to
you for every kind of care they give. Bless
them with your perfect care and armor so
that they too will be renewed in your
peace, health and love by placing their
faith in you Father God and our Lord Jesus.
Amen

Read. Isaiah 40:29-31 God gives strength and
power to those who hope in him
Matthew 11:28-30 Invitation to God's care
Acts 4:10 Healing in Jesus' name
James 5:16 About confession, prayer and
healing

53. FOR FAMILY

Majestic Lord, God of Glory, we thank you with
humble adoration for the blessing of family.
Hold this family in your peace, fill our
hearts with your love and guide our actions
with your wisdom and kindness so that we
live as your family, showing love to others
as to ourselves and honoring your will on
earth as it is in heaven. Amen

Read: 1 Timothy 5:8 About providing for family
Ephesians 6:1-4 About obedience
Psalm 1:1-3 Prosper by delight in God's
word
Matthew 6:9-13 The prayer Jesus taught
Ephesians 2:13-18 God's people are one
family
1 Corinthians 13 Importance of Love

Give

Thanks

54. A BABY IS BORN

God of Life and Love, thank you for the blessing
of this new baby boy or girl. Watch over
his life, light his path and protect his soul.
Let love guide his will and his actions and
give us wisdom and knowledge to care and
educate him to walk in truth on paths that
honor your will. Amen

Read: Psalm 127:3 Children are a gift from God
Luke 18:16 God welcomes children
Proverbs 22:6 Groom children from birth
Deuteronomy 6:6-7 About teaching
children

55. FOR CHILDREN

Shepherd God, King of Love, I lift these children
up to you with gratitude for your divine
gifts of life and love. I ask your
forgiveness for their every failure, for my
flaws and all shortcomings of my care.
With your unmatchable compassion, guide
them, clear their paths, guard their souls
and fill their every hunger so that they
feast at the bountiful table you have
prepared for your chosen and your will be
done forever. Amen

Read: 1 Corinthians 1:4-9 Enrichment from God
Psalm 127:1 Futility without God
Proverbs 22:5-6 Children need guidance
Matthew 19:13-14 Lead Children to God
Deuteronomy 6:5-7 Teach children at every
step
James 3:13-18 About wisdom and good life

56. FOR TEACHERS AND OTHER PROFESSIONS

Exalted Teacher, Holy Father, we are thankful for those who prepare the way for us to travel in truth and knowledge. I ask your grace for those who instructed our goodness, pruned our wildness and corrected our errors and for all who still do. Enlighten them according to your will and grant them peace and joy in their lives as freely as they share their gifts and talents to help others.

Read: 1 Thessalonians 5:12-14 Respect for teachers and caregivers
Mark 1:2-3 Preparing the way of the Lord
Proverbs 1:6-9 About valuing parental teachings
Proverbs 9:9 The wise pursue learning

Give
Thanks

57. A BIRTHDAY PRAYER

Gracious Shepherd, Loving Father in Heaven,
thanks for the blessing of another year to
celebrate your gifts of life, free will,
knowledge and every human need. On this
birthday, I ask that you forgive the wrongs
I have done and help me always forgive
those who do me wrong. Continue to
restore my soul as I walk in the green
pastures of your goodness and guide me
beside the still waters of your peace in this
coming year and always.

Read: Psalm 23 Walking with God
Philippians 4:4-7 Rejoice in the Lord and
find peace
Psalm 1:1-3 A blessing

58. FOR COUPLE CELEBRATING AN ANNIVERSARY

Hallowed Father in Heaven, we celebrate your gift
of abundant joy, love and fellowship that
this couple has enjoyed over their years
together. Thank you for their Holy union,
the treasures they unwrap each day and
the gift of each precious moment that
nourished their marriage like a tree planted
by the water. Accept our gratitude as you
continue to care them to yield fruit in their
season and not wither.

Read: Psalm 1:1-3 Blessing of prosperity
Matthew 12:48-50 Christian family
Proverbs 24:3-4 Wisdom, understanding,
knowledge and home
1 Corinthians 13:4-7 Love perseveres
Isaiah 32:17-20 God's promise for the
righteous home

59. A WEDDING PRAYER

Shepherd of Love, wrap your Holy Spirit into the strands joined by these two. Strengthen their love with your enduring spirit so that they overcome all challenges and flourish with your glory. With your loving grace, shower them with all the joys of a fruitful life together so that their union grows in strength, is refreshed by living water, bears fruit in its seasons and endures by your goodness and mercy forever. Amen

Read: Matthew 18:18-20 Binding together for God
Jeremiah 29:5-7 About settling down
Hebrews 13:4 Honor all marriages
Ecclesiastes 4:9-12 Lives intertwined with God
Ephesians 5:31-33 Care of husband and wife
Psalm 1:1-3 Blessing of prosperity

Pray in the Spirit on all occasions
with all kinds of prayers and requests;
always be alert
and keep praying for all the Lord's people.

Ephesians 6:18

I will pray with my spirit,
but I will also pray with my understanding;
I will sing with my spirit,
but I will also sing with my understanding.

1 Corinthians 14:15

60. A MARRIAGE IN TROUBLE

Lord God, Ruler of the Universe let us feel your sovereign presence in the midst of our trouble. Forgive the wrongs in this couple's lives and help them to let go of the shadows of darkness and find your goodness and light. With your divine mercy, purify their hearts and strengthen the cords binding their lives with your enduring love. Amen

Read: Ecclesiastes 4:9-12 The rewarding cord of marriage
Matthew 11:29-30 Unburden in God's care
Psalm 127:1 Futility without God
Proverbs 4:5-9 Get wisdom and understanding
Matthew 6:12-15 About Forgiveness
1 Corinthians 13 This is Love

Give

Thanks

61. MY FAMILY IS IN TROUBLE

God, Father Almighty, who pleaded to let your
people go from the hands of the ancient
oppressor, save my family from the grip of
this trouble today. Give us wise leadership,
patience and faith to thrive according to
your will the same yesterday, today and
forever. Amen

Read: Hebrews 11:6-7 Act with faith
Hebrews 13:7-8 Unchangeable nature of
God
1 Corinthians 12:27 & 12- Being a member
of a spiritual family
Proverbs 3:21-26 Wisdom keeps you safe
Luke 6:28 Give generously and endure
excessively
Psalm 91:1-2 Refuge in God

Also See: For Family, p.78
And: Someone I Love Disappoints Me, p.68

Give
Thanks

62. MY COUNTRY IS IN TROUBLE

Prince of Peace and Creator of this World, forgive
us our weaknesses and our failure to
fathom what you have done from
beginning to end. Protect your people,
show us the right path and take this
trouble from my country; help us walk with
your light so that your will be done forever,
Amen

Read: Isaiah 1:15-20 Come clean
Ezekiel 14:13-17 About unfaithfulness to
God
Isaiah 54:14-17 God's care for the
righteous
Luke 22:42 Place trust in God's will not
your own
Luke 10:30-37 Compassion vs nationality
1 Peter 2:13-17 Obeying the law
Zechariah 9:8 Patriotism

Give

Thanks

63. A DISASTER OCCURS

Look down on us, O Father of Purest Light. We turn to you with thanks in this dark time, with trust in your forgiveness and hope in your promise of salvation. Shine on your children through this disaster, give us courage and strength and the peace that comes from the care of the one who stilled the waters and calmed the seas to save your people. Amen

Read: Numbers 6:22-27 A Blessing of peace
Psalm 121 Help from God
Romans 14:7-9 Life and death in God's care
Isaiah 45:5-7 God's unlimited power
Ecclesiastes 3:10-12 We cannot fathom God's plan
Mark 4:35-41 Jesus calms disaster

Also see: I Feel Anxious and Worried, p. 26

Give

Thanks

64. MY PEOPLE ARE THREATENED

Omnipotent God, protect my people and deliver
us from this threat of evil. Forgive our
feverish thoughts and ungodly actions and
bless us with wisdom and the gift of your
divine intervention and protection as we as
a people seek favor in your beloved eyes.
Amen

Read: 1 Samuel 2:6-10 God lifts up and brings
down
Ecclesiastes 3:1-8 The changing seasons of
life
Exodus 9:22-30 God saves his people
1 John 1:8-9 Confession and forgiveness
Romans 12:17-21 About revenge
Deuteronomy 20:1-4 Act for God
Hebrews 11: 12-16 A people restored
Matthew 10:26-28 Concern for your soul
Hebrews 12 Work at living in peace
Matthew 10:16 Be shrewd

65. MY SCHOOL IS IN DISTRESS

Lord, Giver of Wisdom and Understanding, I bow before you together with this whole school of people seeking knowledge. We give you thanks for the gifts of school life, seek your forgiveness for our failures and ask your comfort for each of us according to our need. Heal us, quench our thirst at the well of your living knowledge and help us find peace. Amen

Read: Proverbs 8:1-3 & 34-35 Wisdom and understanding bring God's favor
Lamentations 3:31-32 God's compassion
Romans 12:19-21 Leave wrath and vengeance to God
2 Corinthians 1-3-4 Comfort through God's people
John 4:14 & 34 Quenching your needs
Deuteronomy 31:8 Encouragement

66. A PASTOR/ CHURCH LEADER DOES WRONG

Holy and Righteous God, I bow before you to pray for our pastor in his time of weakness. Forgive his wrongdoing, give him strength and understanding and help him to a right path. Heal and comfort your church and give us wisdom, guidance and courage to be as your people through our faith in the Holy Trinity: God the Father, Jesus the Son and the Holy Spirit. Amen

Read: 1 Corinthians 12:28-31 God places various gifted people in the church
Matthew 7:15-23 Recognize false disciples
1 Corinthians 12:21-27 God's workers are equal
Matthew 10:16 Be shrewd
Matthew 18:15-17 Confronting wrongdoers
Matthew 7:2-5 About hypocritical judgement
1 Timothy 3: 1-10 About qualities of leaders
Matthew 18:21-35 About mercy

67. MY CHURCH IS IN TROUBLE

Omnipotent God, at this time of trouble at my
church, I acknowledge our wrongs and ask
that by your grace you forgive us. Reveal
your will for your sorrowful children, inspire
us and prepare us to serve you faithfully
once more to the glory of our savior Jesus
Christ. God's will be done. Amen
[Listen]

Read: Matthew 10:17-23 About trials of the
church
Matthew 5:13-16 God's glory through his
people
Matthew 18:6-9 About removing stumbling
blocks
Psalm 23: God's protection and abundant
provision for his people
Psalm 46:8-11 Be still and observe the
magnitude of God's power

Give

Thanks

68. I WANT TO CHANGE MY LIFE

Oh Lord my God, I kneel before you and ask that
you lead me in your ways. I confess the
many wrongs of my life and ask your
forgiveness, compassion and the gift of a
new life. Teach me, show my heart and
guide me according to your wisdom, I pray
in the name of the Son who came to call
sinners to everlasting life, Amen
[Be Still]

Read: Psalm 25 Entrusting your life to God
Ephesians 2:8-9 Salvation is a gift from
God
Luke 5:32 Jesus calls sinners
Ezekiel 36:24-28 About a new heart and
spirit
1 Peter 2:1-5 God rebuilds lives into
spiritual homes

69. I WANT TO GET CLOSER TO GOD

Divine Lord my God, help me to submit my will to the power of your divine guidance so that I may feel closer to you. Develop my understanding of what you need of my life and my ability to grow with purpose as imperishable seed according to Jesus' word. Amen

Read: Ephesians 5:8-20 Live wisely, enlightened by God
Ephesians 2:8-9 Salvation is by God's grace
1 Peter 1:13-21 Reach for grace above worldly possessions
1 Peter 1: 22-25 Obeying the truth leads to an enduring life
2 Peter 1:3-11 Make these efforts

70. ALL IS WELL

Wonderful Counselor, Mighty God, Everlasting
Father, Prince of Peace, your child gives
you most humble and hearty thanks for
your divine goodness and perfect care for
me and for everyone. I am joyful and
thankful for your light and guidance to use
your cherished gifts for your purposes.
Praise and thanks to God. Amen

Read: 1 Thessalonians 5:15-18 Never stop
praying
Ephesians 5:15-20 About living well
Psalm 145 A song of praise
1 Timothy 2:1-4 Sharing what is good
pleases God

MY ADVENTURE NOTES & SCRIPTURES

ABOUT THE AUTHOR

Karen Sinclair is an Analyst, Researcher and Lay Minister. Her work is inspired by desire to serve others and her prayers are grounded in firm belief that God's will for our lives outshines anything one could ask.

The seed of inspiration for this book was planted years ago by concern that she may not be around to help those she cares about. Her hope is that the book provides a strong anchor for people beset by concern. An advocate for Christian prayer but God's will, she calls readers not to memorize prayers for repetition but to go to God with mindful, personal free will and prayers enriched by understandings from the Bible.

Karen's published books include *Jungle Heart*, a poetic stroll through the emotional jungle of contemporary life; *About Whoever*, a text book exploring the social imprint of identity and orientation; *Little Polka Sock*, a fun fantasy that entertains and educates children; and *The Quiet Sense* which examines the reality of God in a way that today's generations could understand. Her early *Computer Literacy Reference Manual* written at the beginning of the Y2K revolution to help professionals transition to personal computers, was her first book.

Trust in the Lord with all your heart,
and do not lean on your own
understanding.
In all your ways acknowledge him,
and he will make straight your paths.

Proverbs 3:5-6

www.ingramcontent.com/pod-product-compliance
Lightning Source LLC
Chambersburg PA
CBHW061755020426
42331CB00024B/1548